POETRY S⸍

by Typewriter Troubadour

An Interactive Poetry Book
creating Space for Self
Reflection

POETRY SAVES LIVES
Volume I

All Poems Written By Jeremy M. Brownlowe
under the pen name, Typewriter Troubadour.

Artwork by Anthony Carson
Front page photo: Unknown
Back Page Photo: Mara Cook

Font Face: Remington Noiseless

Follow Typewriter Troubadour:

Instagram & Facebook

www.typewritertroubadour.com

www.patreon.com/typewritertroubadour

Typewriter
Troubadour
EST. 2015

Dedicated to those
who bravely explore the shadows
in order to share their light...

It all started with a road trip... and an identity crises. Soon after I hit the road with my typewriter I started a career writing poetry for people in public places.

Driving state to state, typing poem after poem, I found poetry still seemed to resonate with people everywhere. Some folks who stopped at my mobile poetry stand were seeking clarity, hope, love, motivation, empowerment, or simply a reflection of wherever they were at in their life story.

The first time poetry made an impact on me was in the seventh grade. It was right around the time I began to suffer from anxiety and depression (in addition to typical teenage angst). One day a guest came to my English class to show students our words had power, and could be used to express ourselves. For a week straight I could look forward to putting pieces of my soul down on the page, and have been writing in some way ever since.

This person — while I can't remember their name — gave me a huge gift — permission for self reflection... which otherwise is not supported by society. Instead, we are taught to distract ourselves, and stifle any feeling that isn't made out of rainbows.

Such suffering and suppression only leads to feelings of isolation. Writing poetry for various people in various places has taught me that the human condition doesn't vary too much place to place... We all have the basic need to feel safe, seen, heard and loved.

Poetry and creative writing has saved my life countless times, and I hope these poems provide healing to everyone who reads them. Every poem in this collection was written for a stranger in a matter of moments, and hasn't been edited in any way.

There's no doubt society is shifting faster and faster, and we need each other (and poetry) more than ever!

Whether you read cover to cover, or flip through to let the right poem choose you, it's my hope this collection will serve as an interactive guide and provide space for you to reflect on throughout your journey.

Together we CAN make this world a better place. One poem at a time.

— Jeremy M. Brownlowe
Typewriter Troubadour

PSSSST…GET CREATIVE AND COLOR IN THIS ARTWORK BY ANTHONY CARSON (AKA @DRAWINGSBYREQUEST!)

be your true authentic self
    seems so simple
                    so natural
        yet why do we find it so difficult
                at times?
don't let the haters
            and the cannots
        of the world stand in your way
        once you are in the flow
                your dreams will come true
    like magic
            or a bird finally allowed
                    to leave the confines
            of it's cage
                    flying fierce
        into the distance to capture the worm
            without looking back

by ₃mbrownlowe
        san diego, ca
                    june 9th, 2015
        #typewritertroubadour

What I value about my Authenticity:

_____

_____

_____

_____

9

```
believe in what the elders
            have said
                        they have lived
                        and boy are they wise
      believe in the best of others
            for when you give them credit
                        they will truly shine
   believe in nature
            it is strong
                        and is to be respected
   believe in art and words
            for they will save you
   believe in the cause
            for if you don't
                  what are we working towards?
   believe in community
                  it will hold you
                        when you fall back

   believe in yourself
                  for you are a master
                        when you put your mind to it


   by jmbrownlowe
   ojai, ca
   june 14th, 2015
```

What I have learned from my elders:

_____

_____

_____

_____

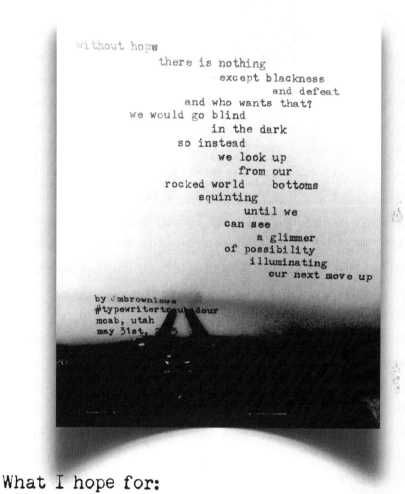

without hope
            there is nothing
                    except blackness
                            and defeat
              and who wants that?
        we would go blind
                in the dark
          so instead
                  we look up
                    from our
        rocked world   bottoms
                squinting
                      until we
              can see
                    a glimmer
              of possibility
                    illuminating
                        our next move up

by Jmbrownlowe
#typewritertroubadour
moab, utah
may 31st, 2025

What I hope for:

_____

_____

_____

_____

Change is the only guarantee in life
            these streets won't look
                the same in ten years time
    no amount of nostalgia can
        prevent the rivers
                    from carving out
    new portals of beauty
        and to stay stagnant
                is death
    the burden of ground hog's day
            the rxxsixinx doors
            keep us moving forward
    xfsx   when one closes
                the mystery
            beyond
        with welcome you
            with more
        than imagination can
            fortell

by JM Brownlowe
            #typewritertroubadour
                pdx, or
        aug 6th, 2015

How Unexpected Change Has Made Life More
Exciting:

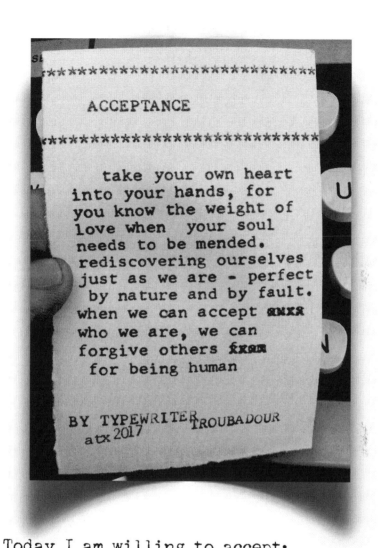

ACCEPTANCE

take your own heart
into your hands, for
you know the weight of
love when your soul
needs to be mended.
rediscovering ourselves
just as we are - perfect
by nature and by fault.
when we can accept ourx
who we are, we can
forgive others from
for being human

BY TYPEWRITER TROUBADOUR
atx 2017

Today I am willing to accept:

_____

_____

_____

_____

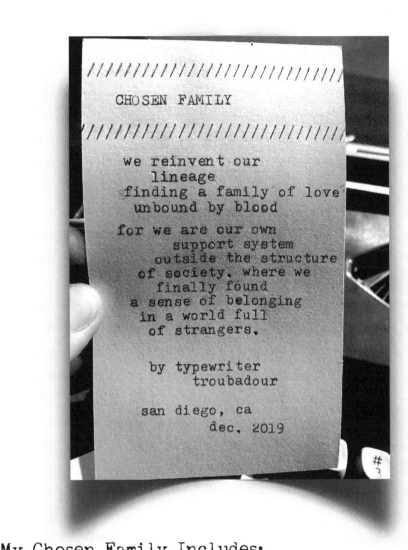

```
/////////////////////////////////

CHOSEN FAMILY

/////////////////////////////////

    we reinvent our
       lineage
   finding a family of love
   unbound by blood

   for we are our own
        support system
        outside the structure
   of society. where we
        finally found
   a sense of belonging
   in a world full
   of strangers.


        by typewriter
            troubadour

        san diego, ca
            dec. 2019
```

My Chosen Family Includes:

_____

_____

_____

_____

//

CLARITY

//

        seeking the source
            of certainty
                that feeling in your
                gut that points
            you to what you know
                to be true ... down
    in the depths of your soul
            a primal guidance
        that helps you make sense
        of the unknown , placingx
    xyax   where the answers come
            after you loosen the grip
        of expectation and control.

    BY TYPEWRITER TROUBADOUR
        SAN DIEGO, CA 2018

Today I seek clarity on:

_____

_____

_____

_____

FORGIVENESS

I cannot carry the weight
        of my pain
                and disappointment
            any longer
    it is a burden,
        a beast,
            who has torn me apart
        I want to forgive the
                fallen angels
            who have proved to be human
                    gnashing teeth
                with cutting words
        for mistakes
                happen
        we hurt the ones
                we love
            it is a curse
                of humanity
        but I can no longer
                carry my own knives
                    and come backs
        it is time for me to
                let go
        to remember why I loved you
                take you back into
                    my arms
                and allow you to be
                        imperfect

by jeremy m brownlowe
    oct 14th, 2015
        #typewritertroubadour
        bend, or

Today I would like to offer forgiveness to:

_____

_____

_____

_____

16

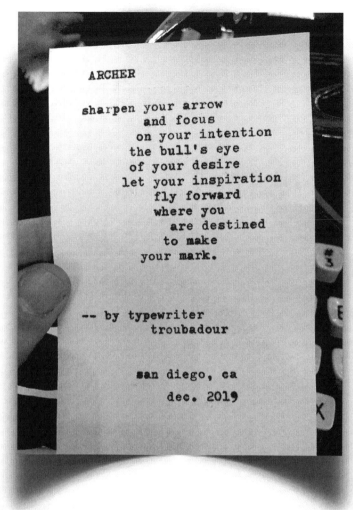

ARCHER

sharpen your arrow
        and focus
        on your intention
        the bull's eye
        of your desire
        let your inspiration
            fly forward
            where you
                are destined
            to make
            your mark.

-- by typewriter
        troubadour

        san diego, ca

        dec. 2019

Goals I can accomplish with focus:

_____

_____

_____

_____

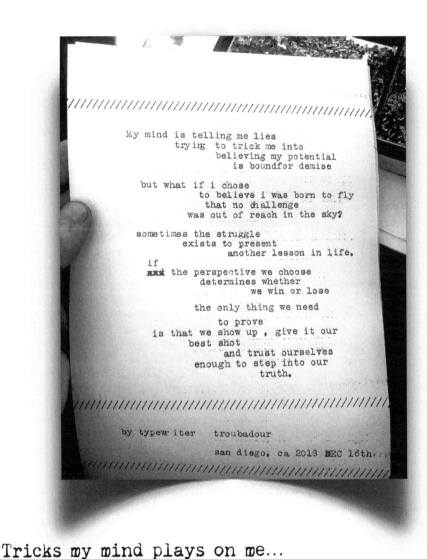

///

My mind is telling me lies
        trying to trick me into
                believing my potential
                    is boundfor demise

    but what if i chose
            to believe i was born to fly
            that no challenge
        was out of reach in the sky?

    sometimes the struggle
            exists to present
                    another lesson in life.
        if
        xxx the perspective we choose
                determines whether
                    we win or lose

            the only thing we need

                to prove
        is that we show up , give it our
        best shot
                and trust ourselves
            enough to step into our
                    truth.

///

    by typewriter   troubadour

                    san diego, ca 2018 DEC 16th.
///

Tricks my mind plays on me...

```
when the dark smokey clouds
          roll in
            and the thunder
                shakes our core
            and we crumble into ourselves
        it is important to summon
            the memory of what we were
                put on this earth to do.
    we are creatures who were meant
                to love
                    to revel in bliss
            and conquer that which
                frightens us
                        like warriors
              fighting against the
                current at times
      however, peace is found
                    in the simplest things
              the heat of the sun
                        kissing our backs
                    golden
              the mist of a walk in spring
        and the kindness we can give
                  and receive
          when we have the bravery
                to break out of ourselves
        and dance with abandon
                        to the music
                  of our precious legacy



              by Jmbrownlowe
                        may 5th, 2015
                  brooklyn, NY
```

My Mission On Earth is...

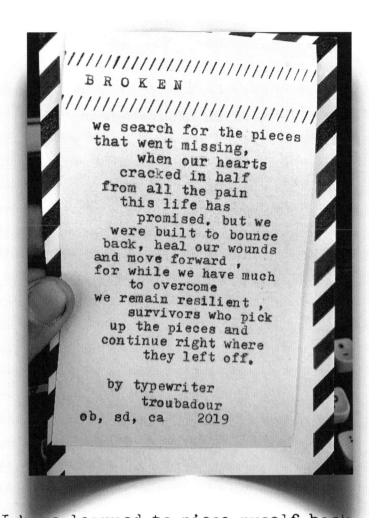

BROKEN

we search for the pieces
that went missing,
when our hearts
cracked in half
from all the pain
this life has
promised. but we
were built to bounce
back, heal our wounds
and move forward ,
for while we have much
to overcome
we remain resilient ,
survivors who pick
up the pieces and
continue right where
they left off.

by typewriter
troubadour
ob, sd, ca   2019

How I have learned to piece myself back
together...

_____

_____

_____

_____

///////////////////////////////////////

darkness.

///////////////////////////////////////

take a walk on the wild
side. simmer amongst the
shadows where   the demons
has gone to rest.
We cannot continue to be
chased by the past
these storms that
shift with the
seasons
and show us where we
have withered
in the depths
of our souls
so someday we can
shift our suffering
to   satisfaction
knowing we have
risen above the storm.

by typewriter
troubadour

Dark moments where I have shined my light:

_____

_____

_____

_____

I am the captain
of my soul ship
steering through
the battering waters
of burden and psyche

Once sick with fear
I have gotten used to
the motion of life
and the intrepid journey
has filled me with confident
excite, ready to conquer
anything in the wake of
my voyage to a future
unknown.

Where I Will Steer My Soul Ship Next:

_____

_____

_____

_____

gratitude
****

we open our eyes to
abundance, shifting our
perspective so we are
no longer scared of
scarcity we are
inspired to share
our blessings
and see how gratitude
is all we need to
surrender to
in order to find inner
peace.

****

by typewriter
troubadour

Today I find gratitude in...

_____

_____

_____

_____

EXISTENTIAL CRISES

a new crises
        crashes in
      whether to break out the knives
            at the fork in the road
            to carve out meaning
            in life
      xxaxxyax inspiring
                the dreamers and the
                seekers
      to question everything.

by typewriter troubadour

        san diego, ca

            may 2018

My current existential query:

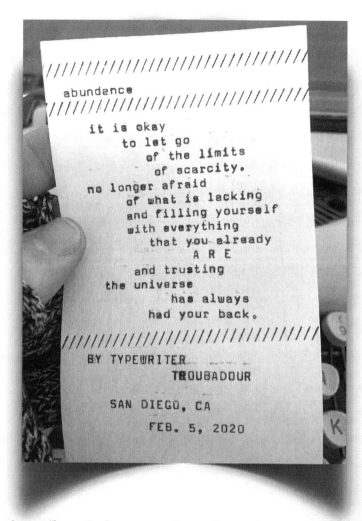

///////////////////////////////
abundance
///////////////////////////////
        it is okay
            to let go
                of the limits
                of scarcity.
        no longer afraid
            of what is lacking
            and filling yourself
            with everything
                that you already
                    A R E
            and trusting
        the universe
                has always
            had your back.
///////////////////////////////
    BY TYPEWRITER
            TROUBADOUR

    SAN DIEGO, CA
        FEB. 5, 2020

Today I celebrate the abundance in life:

_____

_____

_____

_____

There is hope for the future
when we show up with
our best selves -- open
our hearts to new
        possibilities
and understanding.
for when we act with our
    best intentions
        in the present moment
and forgive the mistakes
    and prejudices
    of the past -- we
    have found a solution
    that is destined to
last   and   love   is always
    within our grasp.

    -- Typewriter
        Troubadour

    san diego, ca
    jan. 2020

How I can show up as my best self today:

_____

_____

_____

_____

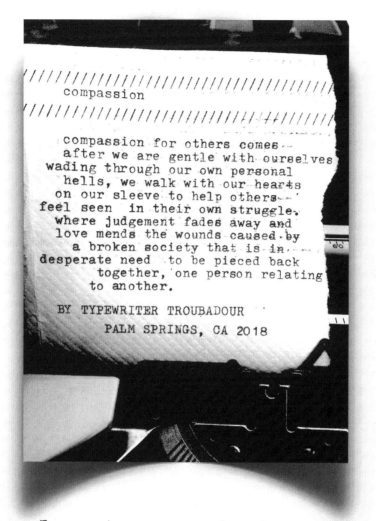

compassion

compassion for others comes
after we are gentle with ourselves
wading through our own personal
hells, we walk with our hearts
on our sleeve to help others
feel seen in their own struggle.
where judgement fades away and
love mends the wounds caused by
a broken society that is in
desperate need to be pieced back
together, one person relating
to another.

BY TYPEWRITER TROUBADOUR
PALM SPRINGS, CA 2018

Ways I can show compassion to myself &
others:

```
DEATH
When the night comes
            it and is all the eyes
                can see
    after a life well lived
        it is time to rest
          the inevitable truth
                    the fate
      of all living beings
                organic
        in their nature
                  we are all
            the same
                  in the end
        when we return
              to wherever it is
                  we came from


  jeremy m brownlowe
      #typewritertroubadour
          pdx, or
        oct. 19, 2015
```

My thoughts on death are:

_____

_____

_____

_____

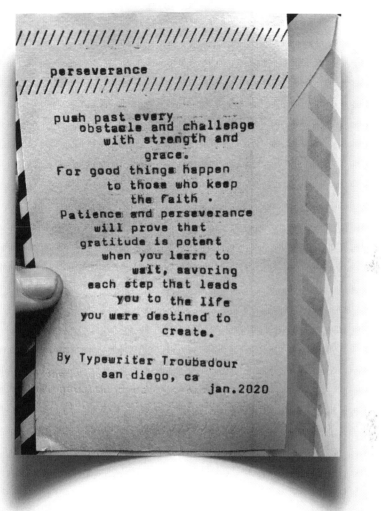

perseverance

push past every
obstacle and challenge
with strength and
grace.
For good things happen
to those who keep
the faith .
Patience and perseverance
will prove that
gratitude is potent
when you learn to
wait, savoring
each step that leads
you to the life
you were destined to
create.

By Typewriter Troubadour
san diego, ca
jan.2020

How I have pushed through challenges:

_____

_____

_____

_____

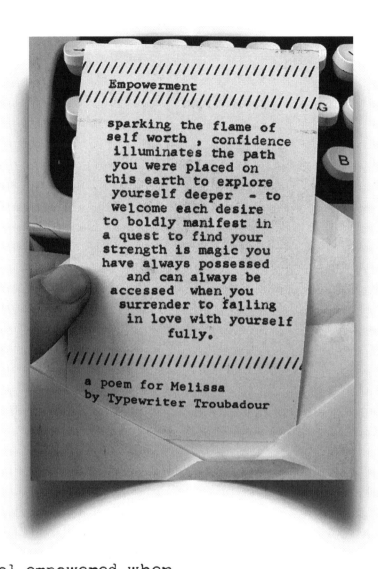

Empowerment

sparking the flame of
self worth , confidence
illuminates the path
you were placed on
this earth to explore
yourself deeper - to
welcome each desire
to boldly manifest in
a quest to find your
strength is magic you
have always possessed
and can always be
accessed when you
surrender to falling
in love with yourself
fully.

a poem for Melissa
by Typewriter Troubadour

I feel empowered when...

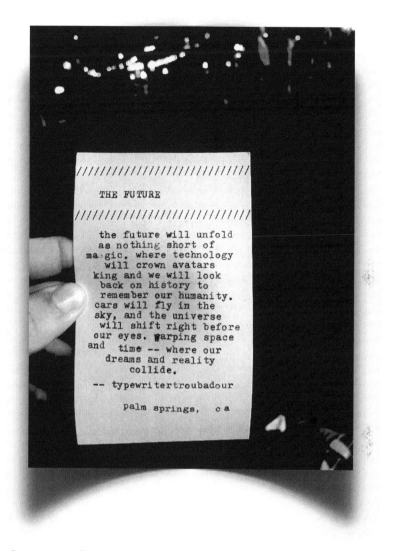

THE FUTURE

the future will unfold
as nothing short of
magic. where technology
will crown avatars
king and we will look
back on history to
remember our humanity.
cars will fly in the
sky, and the universe
will shift right before
our eyes. warping space
and time -- where our
dreams and reality
collide.

-- typewritertroubadour

palm springs, ca

My dreams for the future are...

//////////////////////////////////////

garden

//////////////////////////////////////

she plants the seeds of her desires
nourishing fertile soil
for fruits, veggies and flowers
for she knows the power
of the beauty of a rose
and how much love it --
takes to grow
admire each petal's soft
scent as it fills
the summer night air
with XXX
romance that feeds
her spirit until her hands
are dirty and her heart
is full.

//////////////////////////////////////
ypewriter troubadour
la mesa, ca
july 2019

Simples pleasures in life:

_____

_____

_____

_____

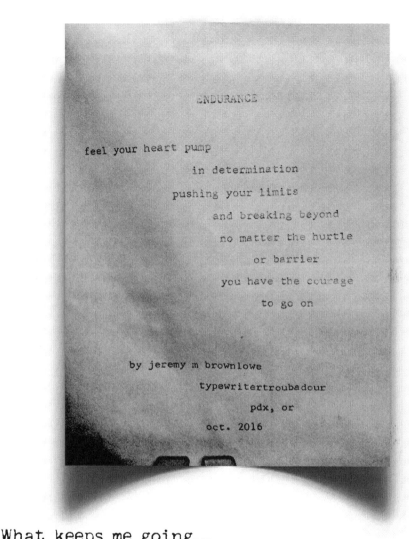

ENDURANCE

feel your heart pump

in determination

pushing your limits

and breaking beyond

no matter the hurtle

or barrier

you have the courage

to go on

by jeremy m brownlowe

typewritertroubadour

pdx, or

oct. 2016

What keeps me going...

_____

_____

_____

_____

recognize genius
but don't forget
        to honor your own.
every artist
    is a critic
they become their own
        enemy
and bask in the glory
        of those who
    became immortal
after they are gonex
already gone.

-- typewriter
        troubadour

    san diego, ca
    jan 2020

I recognize my creativity and inner genius:

_____

_____

_____

_____

FEAR OF THE FUTURE

If the past gets you down
        imagine what the future
        will do
    anxiety levels raising
            red orange
                red
            tipping the scale
                in night sweats
                    and white knuckles
                my teeth grind
                        held tight
            with worry
            and for what?
                the illusion
                    of control
                that I will never have
                        anyways
                    so why confine
                        myself to
                    a fear of the future
                shackled with expectation
        when the best memories of the past
                ware of moments
                        that took me by surprise

            by j.m brownlowe
                typewriter troubadour
                    winter 2015

Surprises that came when I gave up control:

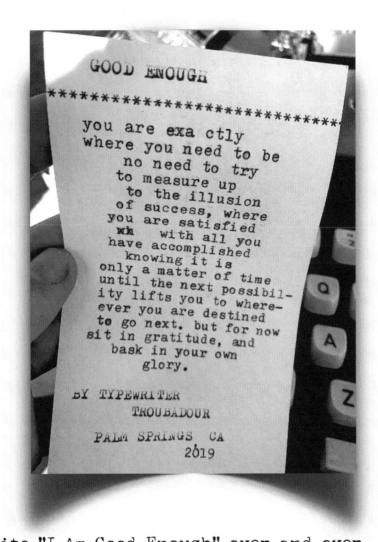

GOOD ENOUGH

****

you are exa ctly
where you need to be
no need to try
to measure up
to the illusion
of success, where
you are satisfied
wk   with all you
have accomplished
knowing it is
only a matter of time
until the next possibil-
ity lifts you to where-
ever you are destined
to go next. but for now
sit in gratitude, and
bask in your own
glory.

bY TYPEWRITER
TROUBADOUR

PALM SPRINGS CA
2019

Write "I Am Good Enough" over and over...

HARMONY

When life is dissonant
and you find yourself
out of scale, strike
a new chord and find
you can serenade your
weary soul. Send
yourself good vibrations
and resonate with
the here and now
and find
when you let yourself
breathe, and slow
yourself down
You will wake up
singing the tune in
the key of gratitude.

BY TYPEWRITER TROUBADOUR

How I bring balance and harmony into my day:

EMPATHY

It is true
    I will never know

        what it means

           to walk

             in your shoes
but I see your pain

    and how you carry yourself

with your head held high
a warrier
    steadfast
and even though I will never

    know exactly how

      the path feels

      beneath

        your feet

I see you march on

    brave

    and know you will

        never be defeated

by jeremy m brownlewe
    typewritertroubadour
pdx, or   nov 2016

I can show empathy to others by...

_____

_____

_____

_____

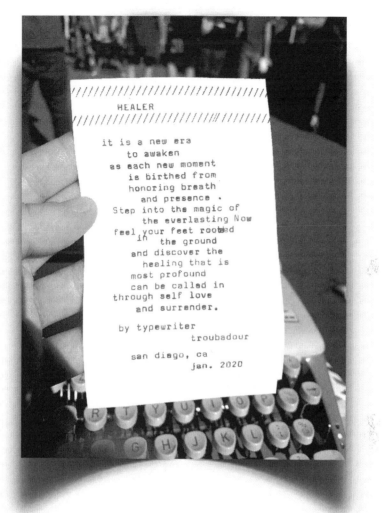

HEALER

it is a new era
to awaken
as each new moment
is birthed from
honoring breath
and presence .
Step into the magic of
the everlasting Now
feel your feet rooted
in the ground
and discover the
healing that is
most profound
can be called in
through self love
and surrender.

by typewriter
troubadour

san diego, ca
jan. 2020

How I can call on my healing guides:

I can hold space for others by...

_____

_____

_____

_____

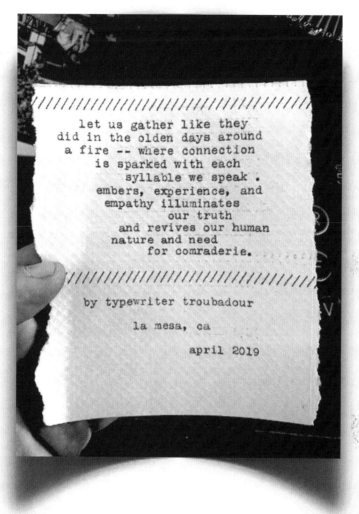

let us gather like they
did in the olden days around
a fire -- where connection
is sparked with each
syllable we speak .
embers, experience, and
empathy illuminates
our truth
and revives our human
nature and need
for comraderie.

by typewriter troubadour

la mesa, ca

april 2019

Ways I can come together with community:

_____

_____

_____

_____

gratitude

when the clouds set in

remember how the rain dances upon

the roof that protects you

or when your heart is in pain

remember you are growing

and had the gift of knowing pleasure

when your soul cries out for more

remember everything you already have

when the darkness
threatens to swallow you

remember the light will return

at dawn

for there is much to be grateful for

a simple pause

a memory

to connect you to the will

of hope

and contentment

by jeremy m brownlowe
typewritertroubadour
oct 2016

pdx, or

Today I am grateful for...

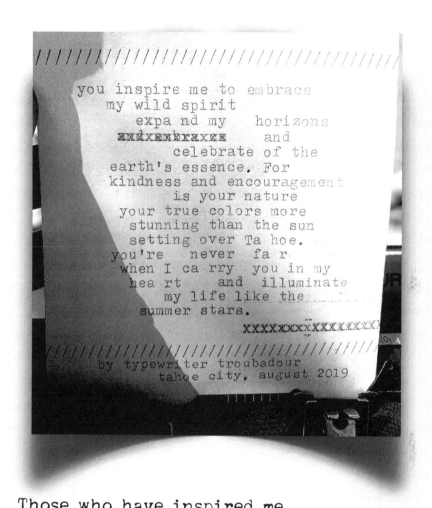

you inspire me to embrace
    my wild spirit
        expa nd my   horizons
    xxdxemkxxxee   and
            celebrate of the
    earth's essence. For
    kindness and encouragement
            is your nature
    your true colors more
        stunning than the sun
        setting over Ta hoe.
    you're   never   fa r
    when I ca rry you in my
        hea rt   and   illuminate
            my life like the
        summer stars.
                    XXXXXXXXXXXXXXX

                by typewriter troubadour
                    tahoe city, august 2019

Those who have inspired me...

_____

_____

_____

_____

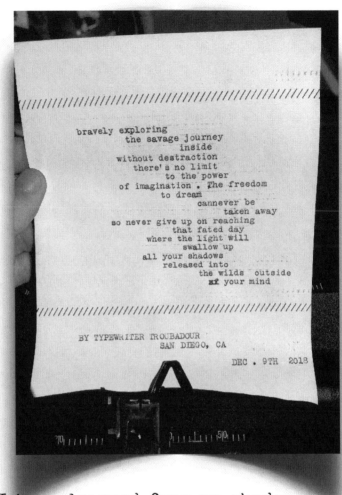

bravely exploring
the savage journey
inside
without destraction
there's no limit
to the power
of imagination . The freedom
to dream
cannever be
taken away
so never give up on reaching
that fated day
where the light will
swallow up
all your shadows
released into
the wilds outside
of your mind

BY TYPEWRITER TROUBADOUR
SAN DIEGO, CA

DEC . 9TH 2018

What I have learned from my shadow:

_____

_____

_____

_____

G O D

///

```
   i see you reflected
            within me
                 the eternal knowing
            that we are one
         creation - a miraculous
                  example of infinity
                  and  unity
         that cradles the
                   entire universe
            and serves as a humble
                   Guide
            as we surrender
                   to spiritual
                      expansion.
```

///

by typewriter troubadour
            palm spring, ca 2019JANU
//////////////////////

My definition of God (other names and
non-secular views are welcome!)

JOY HUNTER

she chooses to seek out the
light , settle
for the simple
delights and open
herself up to satisfying
her senses.
for desire and need
are two different
things - and we
have the tools to sharpen
our knives
to hunt a nd capture
joy wherever we go.

by typewriter troubadour
joshua tree 2019

I seek out joy by...

_____

_____

_____

_____

love and human connection
          is the universal
                    aneddote
        to suffering
    so make eye contact and give
              a nod to the person
        sitting lonesome and weary
                  on the opposite
            subway bench
          compliment the shoes
                  you stare at like magnets
      for kindness is the most
            valuable currency
        and you never know when
              you will make someone
                  wealthy
                        in this respect

          by jmbrownlowe
                  may 5th, 2015
                  brooklyn, NY

I can be kind and helpful to strangers by:

LEAP OF FAITH

we will take our chances
on that the gatekeeper
of the unknown
to place faith
on what we cannot see yet
in tangible reality
our thoughts manifest
our fears and desires
which one will you choose?

by typewriter troubadour
pdx, or 9/3/17

I am willing to take a leap of faith on...

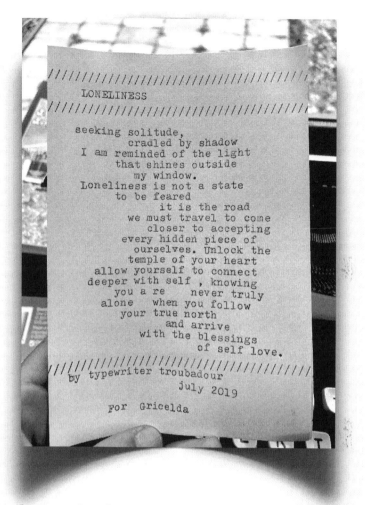

LONELINESS

seeking solitude,
        cradled by shadow
I am reminded of the light
      that shines outside
        my window.
Loneliness is not a state
      to be feared
            it is the road
        we must travel to come
          closer to accepting
        every hidden piece of
        ourselves. Unlock the
        temple of your heart
allow yourself to connect
deeper with self , knowing
      you a re   never truly
      alone   when you follow
        your true north
              and arrive
        with the blessings
                of self love.

by typewriter troubadour
                July 2019

      For Gricelda

What I can do for myself when I'm lonely:

_____

_____

_____

_____

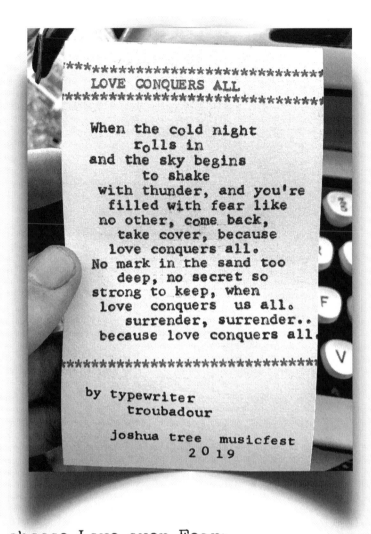

```
************************************
     LOVE CONQUERS ALL
************************************

   When the cold night
        rolls in
   and the sky begins
        to shake
   with thunder, and you're
     filled with fear like
   no other, come back,
      take cover, because
    love conquers all.
   No mark in the sand too
      deep, no secret so
   strong to keep, when
      love  conquers  us all.
       surrender, surrender..
     because love conquers all.


************************************

   by typewriter
      troubadour

   joshua tree  musicfest
          2019
```

Why I choose Love over Fear:

_____

_____

_____

_____

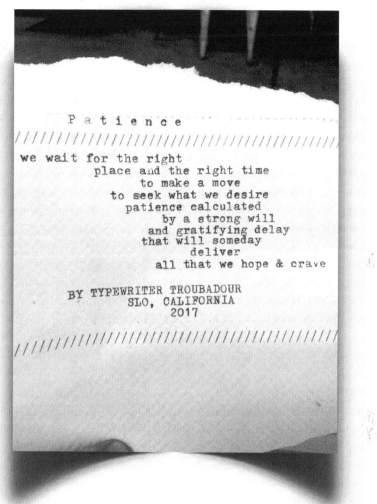

Patience
///

we wait for the right
        place and the right time
            to make a move
        to seek what we desire
            patience calculated
                by a strong will
                and gratifying delay
            that will someday
                    deliver
            all that we hope & crave

BY TYPEWRITER TROUBADOUR
        SLO, CALIFORNIA
            2017

//

How patience has paid off in the past:

_____

_____

_____

_____

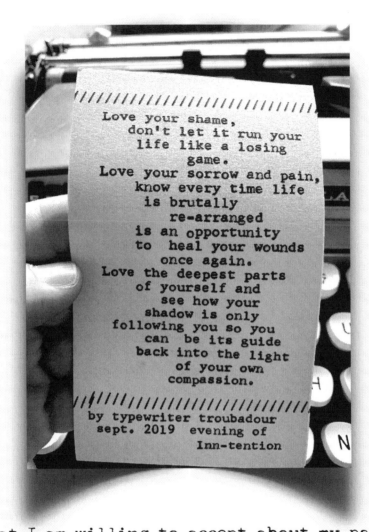

Love your shame,
   don't let it run your
   life like a losing
      game.
Love your sorrow and pain,
   know every time life
      is brutally
         re-arranged
   is an opportunity
   to heal your wounds
         once again.
Love the deepest parts
   of yourself and
      see how your
      shadow is only
following you so you
   can be its guide
   back into the light
      of your own
      compassion.

by typewriter troubadour
sept. 2019 evening of
      Inn-tention

What I am willing to accept about my past:

_____

_____

_____

_____

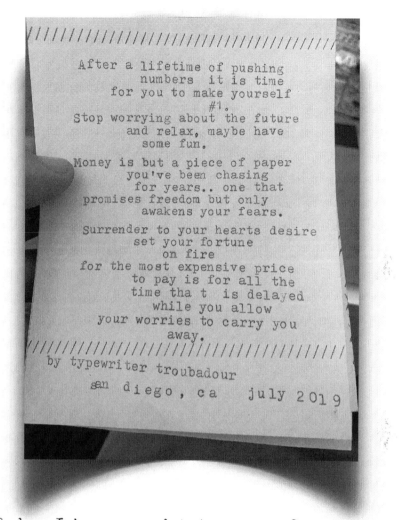

After a lifetime of pushing
numbers it is time
for you to make yourself
#1.
Stop worrying about the future
and relax, maybe have
some fun.

Money is but a piece of paper
you've been chasing
for years.. one that
promises freedom but only
awakens your fears.

Surrender to your hearts desire
set your fortune
on fire
for the most expensive price
to pay is for all the
time tha t is delayed
while you allow
your worries to carry you
away.

by typewriter troubadour
san diego, ca   july 2019

Today I honor and take care of my own
needs by:

Making The Right Choices
///

We always ha ve the choice
to pause, to choose
love at the end
of the day, rather
than fear. We can Honor
our boundaries a nd   needs
and still believe magic
and   is fo und in
understanding the hea rt
of another - someone
who is a reflection of yourself
and serves as a tea cher
or a messenger
of trust , guiding you
to follow your instincts
and find the balance
of abundance and a cceptance
will help us see   our souls
meet ,eye to eye.
///

by typewriter troubadour
san diego, ca
june 2019

Today the next right choice is...

_____

_____

_____

_____

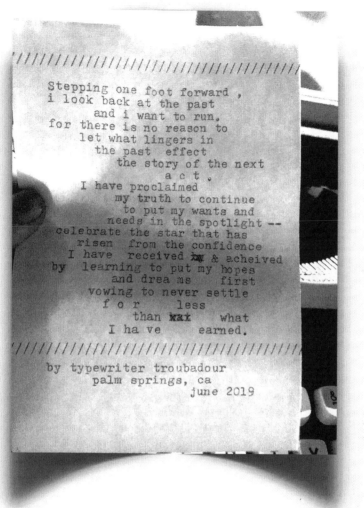

Stepping one foot forward ,
i look back at the past
        and i want to run,
for there is no reason to
    let what lingers in
        the past effect
            the story of the next
                a c t .
I have proclaimed
        my truth to continue
            to put my wants and
                needs in the spotlight --
    celebrate the star that has
        risen from the confidence
    I have received in & acheived
by learning to put my hopes
        and drea ms   first
    vowing to never settle
        f o r   less
            than was   what
    I ha ve   earned.

by typewriter troubadour
    palm springs, ca
                june 2019

Experiences that have given me confidence:

_____

_____

_____

_____

```
/////////////////////////////
The pheonix must burn
  before it learns how to
  fly. Surrender to the
    curiosity to explore the
darkest corridors of your
  mind. All will be right
when you let truth be your
guide. Remember each of the
  shadows can cradle the
  light. Each coincidence
can serve a s  a  sign.
  Trust each serenade will
inspire you to dance in
  your strength. Each bruise
can become a muse who'll
    put your talents to use.
protect your psychic flame
when the clouds bring in
  the rain and let truth
  be  your  only  guide.
/////////////////////////////
BY TYPEWRITER
        TROUBADOUR

  DEC. 2019
```

How I have risen like a phoenix:

_____

_____

_____

_____

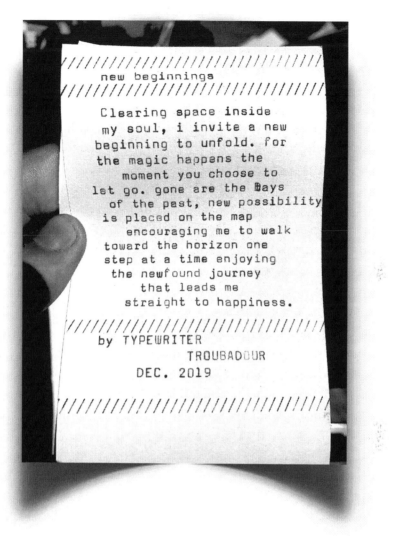

///////////////////////////////////////
   new beginnings
///////////////////////////////////////

Clearing space inside
my soul, i invite a new
beginning to unfold. for
the magic happens the
moment you choose to
let go. gone are the Days
of the past, new possibility
is placed on the map
encouraging me to walk
toward the horizon one
step at a time enjoying
the newfound journey
that leads me
straight to happiness.

///////////////////////////////////////
by TYPEWRITER
          TROUBADOUR
DEC. 2019

///////////////////////////////////////

Blessings that came with new beginnings:

_____

_____

_____

_____

///////////////////////////////////
Sometimes the best thing
to happen to a story is to
start over with a clean slate.
For challenges and tribulation
are the secrets to success
where you are the only
person you need to impress
by finding peace despite
the demons who try and
put you to the test,
before putting you in a
position that
awards you with an
unwavering sense of
self respect.

///////////////////////////////////////

BY TYPEWRITER TROUBADOUR
THE INN AT RANCHO SANTA FE
DECEMBER 2019.

///////////////////////////////////////

What stories no longer serve me...

_____

_____

_____

_____

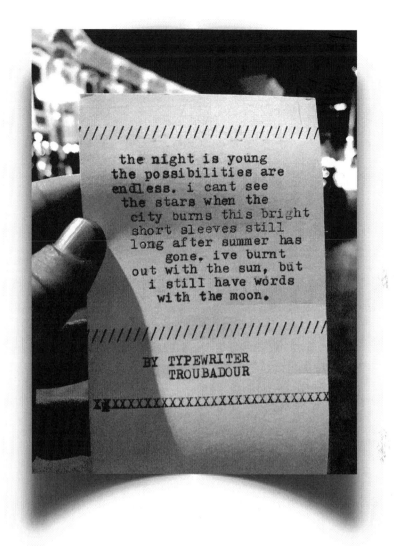

the night is young
the possibilities are
endless. i cant see
the stars when the
city burns this bright
short sleeves still
long after summer has
gone. ive burnt
out with the sun, but
i still have words
with the moon.

BY TYPEWRITER
TROUBADOUR

What makes me feel young at heart:

_____

_____

_____

_____

lately i feel like running
i have the key to my future
burning a hole in my pocket
i've had many holes before
nothing would fill them
not booze
or the perscribed speed
nor herbal remedies
and certainly not women

so i'm running out the door
keys in hand
to drive and see the sights
like i did as a cross country child
this time with fresh adult eyes
and a wandering curiosity

gonna drive drive drive
hands feeling the weight of the wind
out my window
sleeping in tents in the untamed wild
or in the side lots of 24 hour diners
until i reach the familiar faces
who have passed through my town
on their vagabond travels

i thought i would find answers
in the desert dawn
or from the mouths of strangers
though with each mile marker
i become more certain
that i held the key all along
and it was i who was too
afraid to pick at the lock

by jm brownlowe
april 4th, 2015
new orleans

How I have tried to run away from myself
in the past:

_____

_____

_____

_____

```
               R E L A X



  We work hard
            and for what
                 the time
                      we clock
                           out
        and kick back
               to enjoy
                     the
               simple luxuries
         of not having to be anywhere
                 but in the moment
             bathed in relaxation
                  the chaos
                        is still
               and we can learn
                    the basics
                 of breathing
                      ourselves
            back to a state
                    of serenity

   by jeremy m brownlowe
                  typewritertroubadour
           pdx,or
                 may 2016
```

Ways I like to relax...

```
RECEIVE
    THE GIFT
        YOU'VE BEEN SEEKING

1 once met a man
      who told me
         he had a magic ball
              that encased
            the world I desired
                 inside all my
                     hopes and dreams
                and longing
                      would  manifest
              he wanted Me to believe
                 and be open
                 to xxxxxxx  catch
                such magic
         he wanted to throw the ball
                 to me
            so I wouldn't be so
                   lonely in
                 this corner
           only he was wise
                 and looked at me
         with grey eyes
              saying I wasn't able
                     to catch
                such magic
         until I freed my hands
                 from carrying
                     the burdens
              of the past
                    only after I
         let go of what no longer
                served me
           was when I could receive
                 all which I
                 have sought


     by jeremy brownlowe
              #typewritertroubadour
         pdx, or
                 nov. 9th, 2015
```

Gifts I am worthy of receiving...

_____

_____

_____

_____

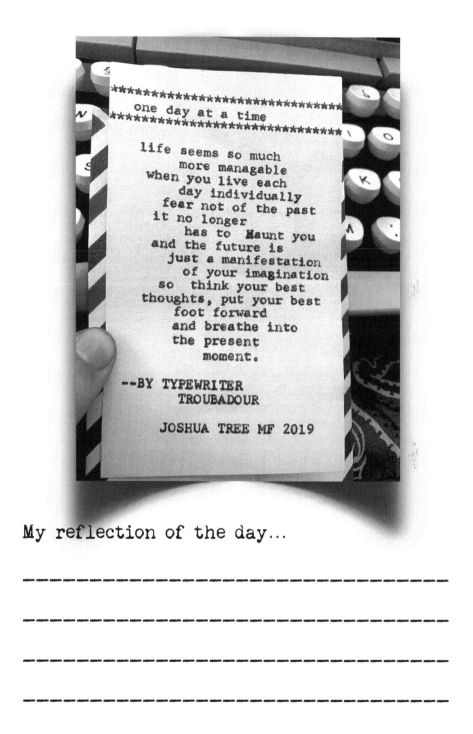

```
*********************************
  one day at a time
*********************************

    life seems so much
          more managable
    when you live each
          day individually
    fear not of the past
    it no longer
          has to Haunt you
    and the future is
          just a manifestation
          of your imagination
    so  think your best
    thoughts, put your best
          foot forward
          and breathe into
          the present
          moment.

  --BY TYPEWRITER
        TROUBADOUR

    JOSHUA TREE MF 2019
```

My reflection of the day...

_____

_____

_____

_____

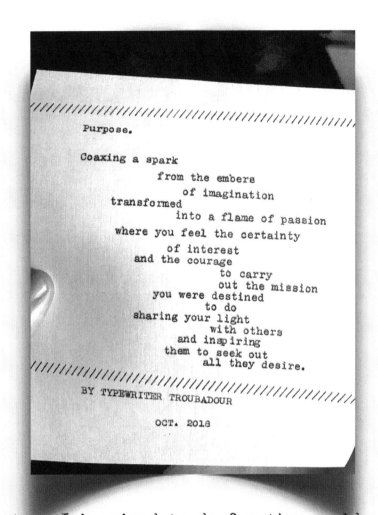

Purpose.

Coaxing a spark
        from the embers
            of imagination
    transformed
            into a flame of passion
    where you feel the certainty
        of interest
    and the courage
                to carry
                out the mission
        you were destined
                to do
    sharing your light
                with others
            and inspiring
            them to seek out
                all they desire.

BY TYPEWRITER TROUBADOUR

OCT. 2018

What am I inspired to do for the world:

_____

_____

_____

_____

NO MORE WAR

When will we stop the blood shed
          sending our men and women
               to do the dirty work
          of the greedy machine
               under a facade of good
     we are starting to open
          our eyes
     see through the lies
and   give a piece of our mind
               to stop
     the charades
          cause no grenade
                    will bring
          peace

by jeremy m brownlowe
          typewriter troubadour
     pdx, or
          jan 7th, 2016

How can I bring more peace to society:

_____

_____

_____

_____

SERENITY

A silence
            has settled within me
                it is the same space
                    where many storms
                        have brewed
                but today is a new day
                        where I can
                    enjoy a piece of quiet
                        a peace within
                a place where I can
                        halt the chatter
                            and the devil's prodding
                and relax into
                        a sacred spell
                            where
                    I can finally sense
                        timelessness
                            in tranquility

by jeremy m brownlowe
    winter 2015
        typewritertroubadour

What brings me serenity:

_____

_____

_____

_____

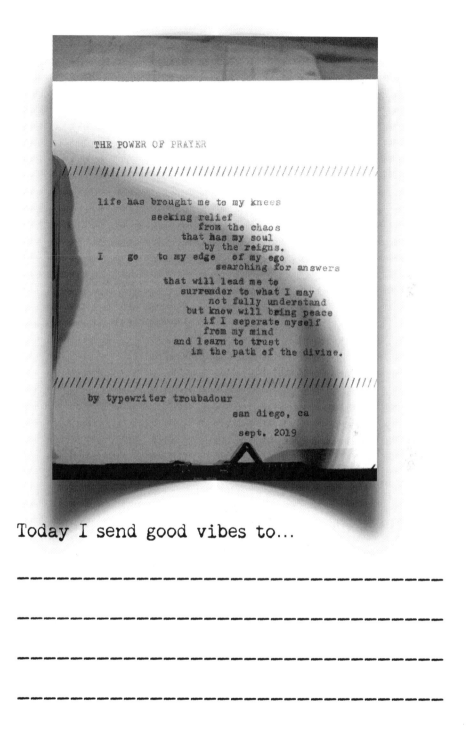

THE POWER OF PRAYER

//

life has brought me to my knees
            seeking relief
                  from the chaos
            that has my soul
               by the reigns.
I   go   to my edge   of my ego
                     searching for answers
            that will lead me to
               surrender to what I may
                  not fully understand
               but know will bring peace
                  if I seperate myself
                  from my mind
            and learn to trust
               im the path of the divine.

//
      by typewriter troubadour

                        san diego, ca

                     sept. 2019

Today I send good vibes to...

_____

_____

_____

_____

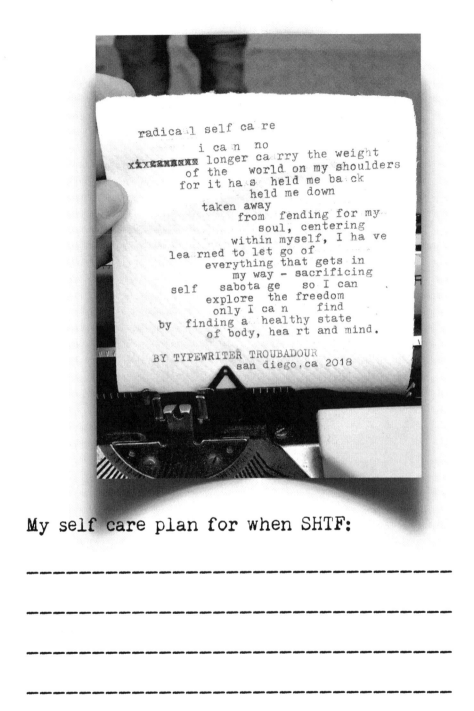

radica l self ca re

i ca n no
xixcanxam longer ca rry the weight
of the   world on my shoulders
for it ha s held me ba ck
held me down
taken away
from fending for my
soul, centering
within myself, I ha ve
lea rned to let go of
everything that gets in
my way - sacrificing
self   sabota ge   so I can
explore the freedom
only I ca n   find
by finding a healthy state
of body, hea rt and mind.

BY TYPEWRITER TROUBADOUR
san diego,ca 2018

My self care plan for when SHTF:

RELEASE

the bats fly from mascara
                clad eyes
          tears of glory
                          streaming down my face
             i n victory
                          the throb
          in my chest broken
             and pumping back tolife
                through sorrow
             pants
     we have been taught not to release
                our demons
          instead to swallow them
             feed them
                anger
          hoping whiskey
                          will kill them
             steralize the pain
          from the needle
                     the obnoxious poke
          of society's burden
     forgetting we do have the power
                to set ourselvesfree
          simply by feeling
                     what sets out
          to destroy our insides
                                anew
     by j.m brownlowe

             pdx, or   #typewritertroubadour

                     aug 27th, 2015

Healthy ways to release, process, or feel
my emotions:

_____

_____

_____

_____

HEALING

```
the wounds
         we sit with
                   are proof that we are alive
                        dealing
                   with the trials
                           of the world
         our hearts
                   start off fragile
                        then become stronger
                                with each pulse
                        taking life as it comes
                            learning
                   growing
                        into
                   a warrior
                        whose wounds
                   have healed into scars
                        that triumphantly
                   remind us
                            what we were able
                               to handle

         a poem by jeremy m brownlowe
                   typewritertroubadour
                        pdx, or
                   may 2016
```

Scars I carry that remind me of my
strength:

70

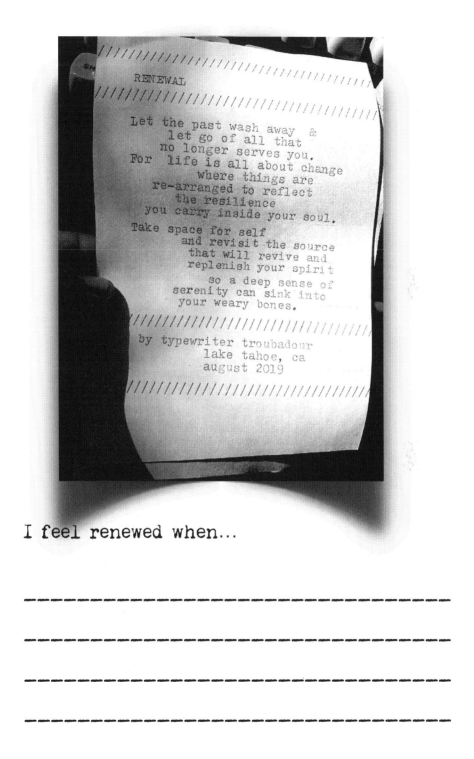

RENEWAL

Let the past wash away &
let go of all that
no longer serves you.
For life is all about change
where things are
re-arranged to reflect
the resilience
you carry inside your soul.

Take space for self
and revisit the source
that will revive and
replenish your spirit
so a deep sense of
serenity can sink into
your weary bones.

by typewriter troubadour
lake tahoe, ca
august 2019

I feel renewed when...

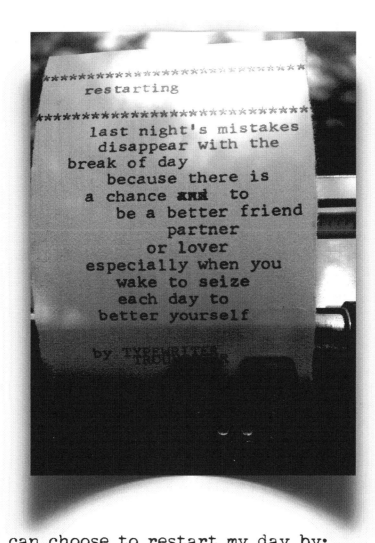

```
*******************************
   restarting

*******************************
   last night's mistakes
   disappear with the
 break of day
      because there is
 a chance and to
    be a better friend
         partner
       or lover
  especially when you
     wake to seize
     each day to
   better yourself


by TYPEWRITER
    TROUBADOUR
```

I can choose to restart my day by:

_____

_____

_____

_____

SELFLESS

To see outside
          to give a shirt
                and an ear
          to help
                unconditionally
              Setting
        the ego aside
              to be present
          to show up
                for another
              without
              expectation
                  a safe guard
              for you I
                will take a stand
              solely because
                  I care
              my only
                  mission
                          in life
              is to love you

by jeremy m brownlowe
        #typewritertroubadour
        pdx, or
        oct 16th, 2015

How others have helped me by being
selfless:

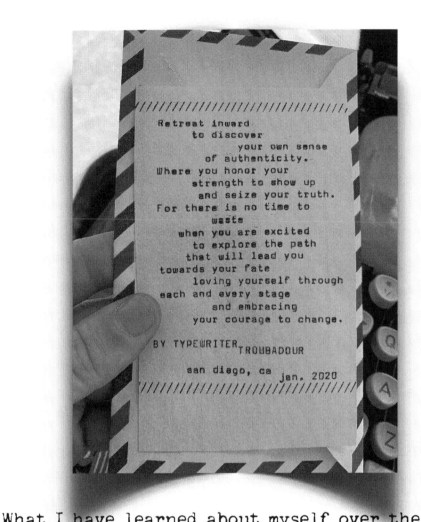

Retreat inward
    to discover
        your own sense
    of authenticity.
Where you honor your
    strength to show up
    and seize your truth.
For there is no time to
        waste
    when you are excited
    to explore the path
    that will lead you
towards your fate
    loving yourself through
each and every stage
    and embracing
    your courage to change.

BY TYPEWRITER TROUBADOUR

san diego, ca jan. 2020

What I have learned about myself over the years:

_____

_____

_____

_____

shave your head
in response to the
patriarchy
wear toe rings like
it is 1969
and always keen
sharpening
that Revolutionary
mi nd

BY JEREMY
      AKA TYPEWRITER
            TROUBADOUR
(akaa the OUTLAW POET)
oceanside, california
2017

Ways I can help create a new paradigm:

_____

_____

_____

_____

RIGHT   NOW

///

right now is all we have
          so we may as well
                     be ourselves
          staying pure in our truth
     we shout our opinions
          proud
for we stand
          with our feet on the
               ground
     we take in the moment
          whether silly or profound.

///

by TYPEWRITER TROUBADOUR

PHILLY 2018

///

I appreciate about life right now:

_____

_____

_____

_____

```
*******************************
        sanctuary
*******************************

        She sets her intention
     to reinvent her space
          so it is a sanctuary
          of serenity. clearing
     space for silence and
          peace of mind, so she
     can hear the messages
       of the divine
          and connect deeper
          to the true beauties
       of      life.


*******************************
       by typewriter
          troubadour

     an evening of Inntention
          sept. 2019
```

What is my safe place or sanctuary:

//

SERENITY   & ANXIETY

//

```
i   ca n     steer
                the ship of my soul
              through the storm
          when the wind of my worries
                 begins to howl
                I know centering
        in    my      breath
                  is how i can
              connect to the ground
              for suffering
                   is an awakening that
                   is profound.
         anxiety and stress
               you are  my greatest
                         teachers
              for you create space
                  for me to become
                   my greatest healer.



         by typewriter troubadour
                  venice, ca
                       sept. 2019
```

//

How can stress serve as my teacher:

//

Slow down to
       xxxx savor ea ch   step
              of the street fa ir
Slow down
       to   take in a Brea th
              of fresh air
For there is so much
       to be grateful for
          when we open our eyes.
Heaven doesnt ha ve to be a place
       in the sky,
          when I got my babies
          and my man
       by my side
          I am surrounded
                 by pure love
                 and light.
Be here with me now,
       shout your love outloud
          Slow down..
          Slowx down..
          Slow   down..
//
by typewriter troubadour
          la mesa, ca
                 may 31, 2019

The benefits of slowing down are...

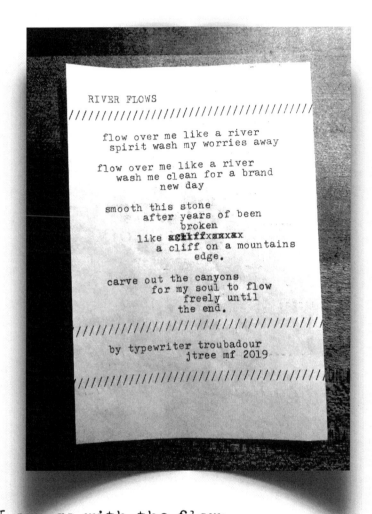

RIVER FLOWS
//

flow over me like a river
    spirit wash my worries away

flow over me like a river
    wash me clean for a brand
            new day

smooth this stone
        after years of been
            broken
        like xcliffxxxxxx
        a cliff on a mountains
                edge.

carve out the canyons
    for my soul to flow
        freely until
        the end.

//////////////////////////////////////
        by typewriter troubadour
            jtree mf 2019
//////////////////////////////////////

How I can go with the flow:

_____

_____

_____

_____

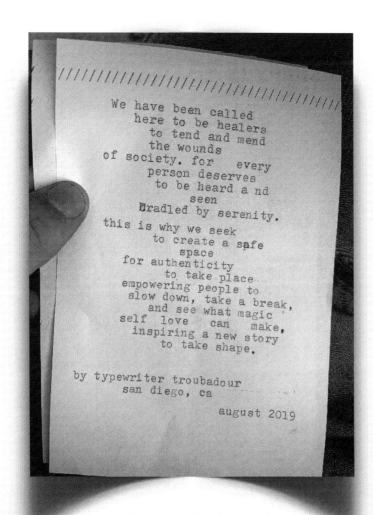

We have been called
here to be healers
to tend and mend
the wounds
of society. for   every
person deserves
to be heard a nd
seen
cradled by serenity.

this is why we seek
to create a safe
space
for authenticity
to take place
empowering people to
slow down, take a break,
and see what magic
self love   can   make,
inspiring a new story
to take shape.

by typewriter troubadour
san diego, ca

august 2019

What I can offer to help others on their
journey:

_____

_____

_____

_____

We remind each other
        of the magic
    we carry inside
blessings so often missed
        by the blink
    of the modern eye.
we have gone through
        an oddyssy
      reincarnated
            as a butterfly
    kissing each flower
      hello and goodbye
knowing the secret of
        the season is sacred
              temporary
    in the consciousness
        of time.

by typewriter troubadour
    palm springs, ca
        3/7/2019

What is beautiful about this season of
life?

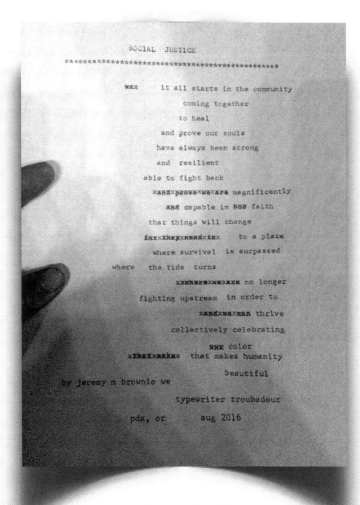

SOCIAL JUSTICE

****

wwx   it all starts in the community

coming together

to heal

and prove our souls

have always been strong

and resilient

able to fight back

xxxxxprovexwexare magnificently

and capable in xxx faith

that things will change

fxxxthexxmxxndxxxx   to a place

where survival is surpassed

where the tide turns

xxwxheraxwexxxx no longer

fighting upstream in order to

xxxdxxexxxx thrive

collectively celebrating

xxx color

xthxxxxxkxx that makes humanity

beautiful

by jeremy m brownlo we

typewriter troubadour

pdx, or   aug 2016

How can I be an advocate for marginalized communities?

_____

_____

_____

_____

```
SOLIDARITY


When we join together
        despite our differences
              and the tired old story
        we are unstoppable
            we move fast
                and strong
                like a freight train
                    barrelling down the tracks
          our path is set
                towards unity
                      the soliders for humanity
              need not weapons
                  but rather
                  their hands from   unclenched of war
            XXX       to catch
                            and disperse
                        the miracle
                    of freedom
                    and the celebration of many selves
                                a well oiled machine
        by jeremy m brownlowe
              typewriter troubadour
              pdx, or
              dec. 14th, 2015
```

The benefits of coming together in society:

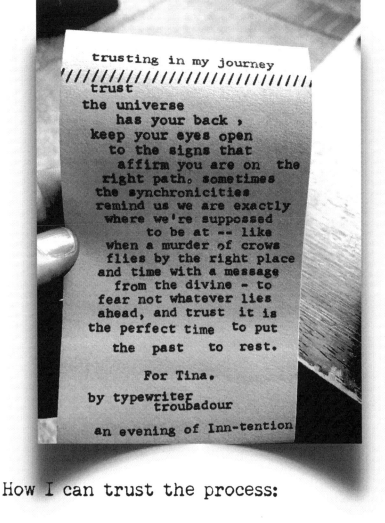

trusting in my journey
//////////////////////////////
trust
the universe
    has your back ,
keep your eyes open
    to the signs that
        affirm you are on the
right path. sometimes
the synchronicities
remind us we are exactly
where we're suppossed
        to be at -- like
when a murder of crows
flies by the right place
and time with a message
    from the divine - to
fear not whatever lies
ahead, and trust it is
the perfect time to put
        the past   to rest.

        For Tina.

by typewriter
        troubadour

an evening of Inn-tention

How I can trust the process:

_____

_____

_____

_____

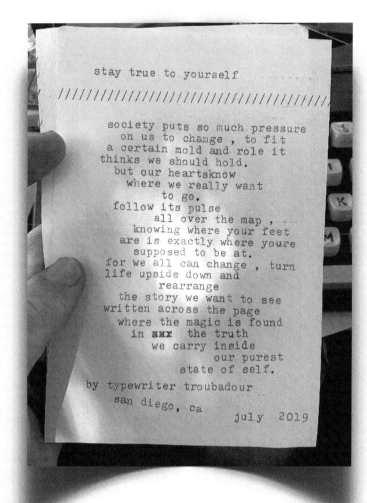

stay true to yourself

///

society puts so much pressure
on us to change , to fit
a certain mold and role it
thinks we should hold.
but our heartsknow
where we really want
to go.
follow its pulse
all over the map ,
knowing where your feet
are is exactly where youre
supposed to be at.
for we all can change , turn
life upside down and
rearrange
the story we want to see
written across the page
where the magic is found
in ☒☒ the truth
we carry inside
our purest
state of self.

by typewriter troubadour
san diego, ca

july 2019

I can honor others, and stay true to
myself by:

```
strength
          lies in the soldiers
              inside your chest
          a love that cannot
              be caged
          when there is a mission
              to triumph
                  and transcend
              a yearning
                  a calling
              so vital
                  in honor
          touching everyone
              within your
                  sight
          and strong willed
                  reach
          to do the right thing
              always
                  with an open
                  mind
          and tender heart
              that beats
          so fierce and solid
              leading those
                  within earshot
          back to the source
                  of its echo
```

[signature]

by jeremy m brownlowe
typewriter troubadour
winter 2015

Examples of my strength:

_____

_____

_____

_____

Surrender
    and put down the
sword you have pointed
at yourself in the
        mirror.
Learn to love yourself
    unconditionally
        and step straight
            into your fear.
Embrace the bravery
    that is needed
        to welcome change.
For this is how the path
    to victory is paved.

BY TYPEWRITER
        TROUBADOUR

San Diego, CA
    JAN. 2020

Today I am willing to surrender by letting
go of...

_____

_____

_____

_____

```
***********************************************************

                Sink your fingers
                        into the earth
                  to find the root
                            that will grow
                  to fruition
                            with a little care
                  and patience
              like the breath
                            you have learned
                  to train steady
                    in your practice
                            that helps you
                  reach zen
              and the enlightenment
                    gifted to you
                  by the sun and the spirits beyond
***********************************************************

        by jeremy m brownlowe

                    typewriter troubadour
            pdx, or                        aug 2016
```

I find my inner zen when...

_____

_____

_____

_____

```
*********************************
This Is It
*********************************

      life is the greatest
    gift. so let us remember
    to open up our hearts
       and live every day like
    a work of art. let us
       remain   rooted  in
       each moment, sacred and
    unique, where we take
       a d v a n t a g e  of
       every breath we breathe.
    For there is no time to
    waste when we can be
    chasing after our dreams ,
       and bring everything
    we imagine  into this
       temporary  state  of
            reality.


    ** TYPEWRITER
       TROUBADOUR

    OCT. 2019
```

What's on my bucket list?

_____

_____

_____

_____

```
///////////////////////////////
        t i m  e
///////////////////////////////
        time is moving faster
        so it seems. time is
        a myth that measures
          the expansion of this
        galaxy. the past isnt
           anything but a memory
        and the future is an
        illusion crafted by
        a curious imagination.
         time - the currency
        that we cannot claim
        but will claim us in
           the end. so enjoy
        the present moment
     a s      Each second ticks
         by , savoring each
        breath and the momentum
        of the clocks hand
           while you can.

        by typewriter
             troubadour

              ob    2 019
```

How do I want to spend my time?

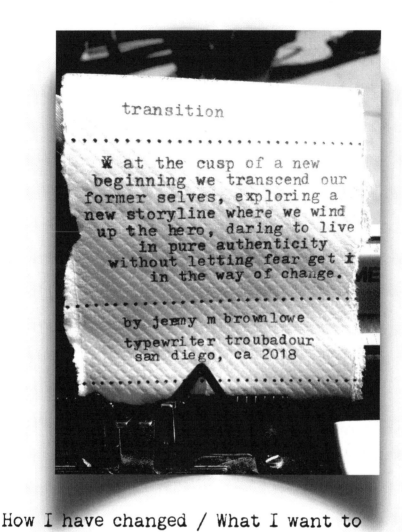

transition

W at the cusp of a new
beginning we transcend our
former selves, exploring a
new storyline where we wind
up the hero, daring to live
in pure authenticity
without letting fear get i
in the way of change.

by jenny m brownlowe
typewriter troubadour
san diego, ca 2018

How I have changed / What I want to change:

_____

_____

_____

_____

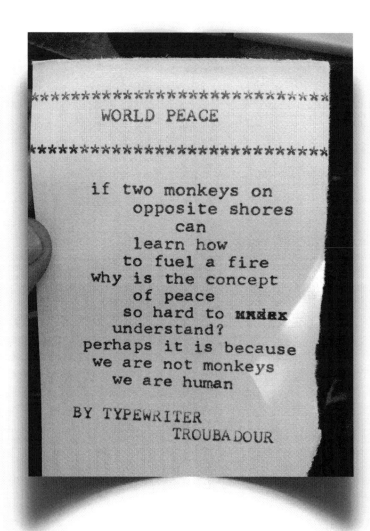

```
**********************************
        WORLD PEACE

**********************************

      if two monkeys on
           opposite shores
               can
           learn how
         to fuel a fire
     why is the concept
          of peace
        so hard to xxxxx
       understand?
     perhaps it is because
     we are not monkeys
       we are human

   BY TYPEWRITER
              TROUBADOUR
```

How can humans consciously evolve?

_____

_____

_____

_____

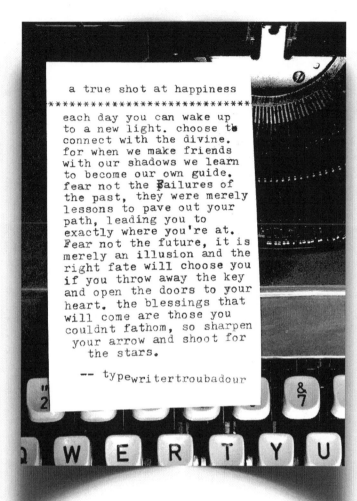

a true shot at happiness

****

each day you can wake up
to a new light. choose to
connect with the divine.
for when we make friends
with our shadows we learn
to become our own guide.
fear not the failures of
the past, they were merely
lessons to pave out your
path, leading you to
exactly where you're at.
Fear not the future, it is
merely an illusion and the
right fate will choose you
if you throw away the key
and open the doors to your
heart. the blessings that
will come are those you
couldnt fathom, so sharpen
your arrow and shoot for
the stars.

-- typewritertroubadour

What makes me happy:

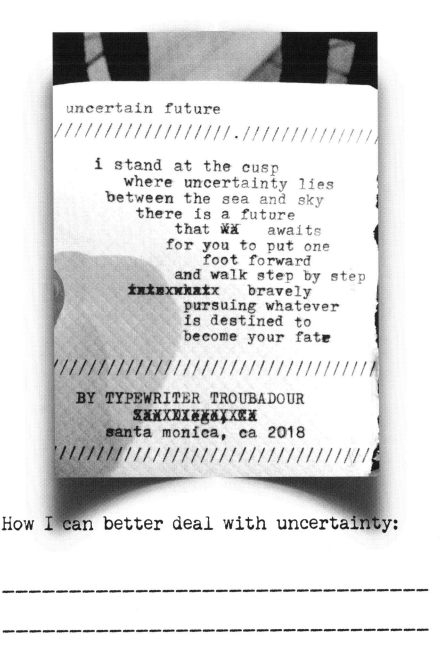

uncertain future

///////////////////.////////////////

i stand at the cusp
where uncertainty lies
between the sea and sky
there is a future
that ~~WX~~ awaits
for you to put one
foot forward
and walk step by step
~~intexwhatx~~ bravely
pursuing whatever
is destined to
become your fate

//////////////////////////////////

BY TYPEWRITER TROUBADOUR
~~XXXXXXXXXXXX~~
santa monica, ca 2018

//////////////////////////////////

How I can better deal with uncertainty:

_____

_____

_____

_____

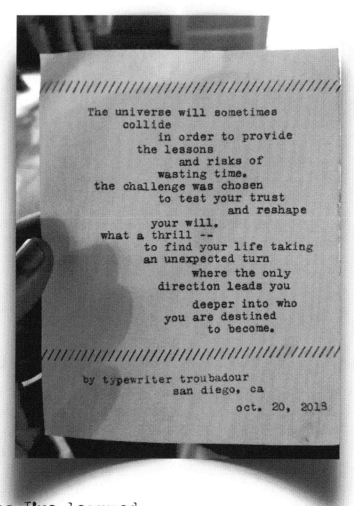

The universe will sometimes
        collide
            in order to provide
        the lessons
            and risks of
        wasting time.
the challenge was chosen
        to test your trust
                and reshape
        your will.
what a thrill --
        to find your life taking
        an unexpected turn
                where the only
        direction leads you

                deeper into who
        you are destined
                to become.

by typewriter troubadour
        san diego, ca

                oct. 20, 2013

Lessons I've learned...

_____

_____

_____

_____

artists and philosophers
have a new query on their hands
how,when the world is being
swallowed
by machines,
are we to remain human
in the end?
xfor to craft and to create
with a stroke of a pen
feeling the tangible nature
of your soul coming from
the divine hand
leaving relics and remains of
what it once meant
to be human.

typewriter
troubadour

potland, or
aka portland

april 201

A Poem By
JEREMY M. BROWNLOWE

How can humans hold onto their humanity
in the age of technology?

_____

_____

_____

_____

```
                U T O P I A


    I pray
          utopia
                isn't a myth
                    nor a mirage
                because I am thirsty
                    for understanding
                        and kindness
                            in this world
              who seems to be under
                            a relentless
                                heat
              why must such a notion
                    be rendered
                        to fiction

                xjxxtxxxxtk
                  perhaps
        once the thirst
                for connection
                        is undeniably
                            unquenched
                    upon our txxxg
                            tongues
                  is the point
                      where
                  we will dare to swim
                      out into the lawless sea
            xxdxdxxgxmxxxxxxxfxxmxxtkxxtxtxxd
                xxxxxxkxxkxxxx
        by jeremy m brownlowe
              typewriter troubadour
                    may 2016
                  pdx, or
```

My vision of utopia:

_____

_____

_____

_____

remember the time when you
        were a kid and your imagination
        was your best friend
        and a trampoline could actually
        help you reach the stars or
so it seemed until gravity set in
        and your dreams came crashing down
        or the more questions you asked
        only led to more forks in the path
        the route less traveled
        or the cage of a safety net
                these are the questions
        that keep us up at night tossing
    and turning yearning for a simpler
        time when we didn't have to
        think so much

        by jeremy m brownlowe
            typewritertroubadour
                pdx, or
                    nov 2016

How can I connect with my inner child?

_____

_____

_____

_____

Be here now
        those are the words
                of the wise
        the enlightened
                and the pulse of the sacred
    for this moment is all we have
                the past is behind us
        what is done is done
        the future is an illusion
            what will happen
                        will happen
        and doesn't need our worry
    so open your eyes
                    wherever you are
        and embrace all your senses
                and the world around you
        for who knows what you will
                    see
                perhaps for the very first time

        by Jmbrownlowe
            may 6th, 2015
            brooklyn, NY

| 30 | 40

What I notice ... right NOW...

FREEDOM

****

though we are human

we have wings

that must never be clipped

we wish to taste the freedom

of the sky

where there are no limits

where every soul

is able to soar

and reach great heights

of their potential

this must not be Reduced to

a dream

- the dream of flying -

this is why we

march together on the ground

to demand ᴍᴍxᴍᴍ

ᴍᴍ   everyone be released

from the cage ɢfxᴍᴍᴋᴋ

society has tried to ᵽᴋxᴋ

keep   them in

by jeremy m brownlowe   typewritertroubadour

pdx, or   july 2016

What life will look like when everyone is free:

_____

_____

_____

_____

Jeremy M. Brownlowe is no stranger to his shadow.

Besides writing custom poems as Typewriter Troubadour he finds inner peace by writing stories of self reflection.

Other titles include:

Angels Of The Underground (2018)
Typewriter Troubadour Anthology (2015-18)
Storybook Girlfriend (2020)

He is currently based in Southern California, splitting his time between San Diego, Palm Springs and Joshua Tree.

Read More Online:
www . patreon . com / typewritertroubadour

More Space to Create:

Made in the USA
Columbia, SC
20 August 2023

21822505R00063